Why Dogs Don't Worship God

By Sarah Taggart

AuthorHouse™
1663 Liberty Drive, Suite 200
Bloomington, IN 47403
www.authorhouse.com
Phone: 1-800-839-8640

© *2009 Sarah R. Taggart. All rights reserved.*

No part of this book may be reproduced, stored in a retrieval system, or transmitted by any means without the written permission of the author.

First published by AuthorHouse 2/5/2009

ISBN: 978-1-4389-3426-6 (sc)

Printed in the United States of America
Bloomington, Indiana

This book is printed on acid-free paper.

Taggart copyright 2008

For Lillie

Table of Contents

Preface xi

Introduction xiii

Chapter One The Human Animal 1

Chapter Two When Science is not Scientific 9

Chapter Three Creatures With Souls 17

Chapter Four Communicating with God 23

Chapter Five The Devil In The Details 35

Chapter Six The Great Unknowable 45

Chapter Seven Christian Metaphors 53

Chapter Eight Beauty, Truth and Goodness 59

Chapter Nine God In The Details 67

Epilogue God at the Fringes of Science 75

I never saw a moor

I never saw the sea.

Yet know I how the heather looks

And what a wave must be.

I never spoke with God

Nor visited in heaven

Yet certain am I of the spot

As if the chart were given.

-Emily Dickinson

Preface

This book is my response to my sixteen year old granddaughter's anguished confession that she no longer believes in God, even though she attended a Presbyterian Sunday school from her earliest years. Her Sunday school had never addressed her primary religious questions: Does God exist? and Why ought we to care?

I take on those two questions. The book is written for young people, but I hope that it will also answer adult questions as well. I try to simplify fundamental ideas and I deliberately include some "New Age" stories in an effort to expand curiosity and provoke arguments.

I am that most inquisitive and skeptical of believers, an adult convert to belief. No one in my family believed in God—not one person. So I have spent fifty years answering my own questions (God spent fifty years answering my questions) and exploring different churches.

In developing this book I owe thanks to Lillie Taggart, Bruce Taggart, Sondra Willobee, Dick Henderson, Gabriel Weinreich, Norma

Kumbier, Vicki Stewart, Lois Perry and Mary Lu Fennell. Readers will also find many references to the influential Christian apologist, C. S. Lewis.

I have a Doctor of Ministry degree, and have written three books about my religious quest: *The Elephant Called Reality* (Dissertation: The Ecumenical Theological Center 1990), *Living As If* (Jossey-Bass 1994) and *Searching For Dr. God* (Authors Guild Reprint 2008). I am married and have three sons and six grandchildren.

Introduction

Congress shall make no law respecting an establishment of religion, or prohibiting the free exercise thereof. (United States Constitution: First Amendment)

You probably learned atheism in public school.

Of course, that's not what it was called. It was called "religious neutrality." But two hundred years after it was adopted, the Establishment of Religion clause (above) has been interpreted to mean that religious beliefs are neither presented nor discussed in school. At all. You will not find the word "God" in text books. (Check it out in their indexes.) Separation of church and state is enforced in our schools by an intellectual wall without doors or windows. As a college teacher I experienced it, and as a grandparent I listened to my grandchildren struggle with it.

Why does it matter? Not, as superstitious people say, because when you turn your back on God you get what you deserve. It matters because when you turn your back on God, you think you are God and can do whatever you like. Who cares if you "look out for number one"? Who cares if your parents are good to you, or if spending money is the best way to be happy? Or, in fact, who cares if you don't take care of yourself, or are mean to your children? If there is no God, mostly we care because we might get caught, or our friends might not like us. If there is no God. . . . I don't need to go on, because our whole society is based on the fundamental assumption that there is no God.

Making progress:

A hundred years ago someone suggested that "every day in every way we are getting better and better." It seemed obvious. But is it true? Are we in the twenty first century better than people were in (let's say) the nineteenth century? Certainly we know much, much more, and therefore we can accomplish much, much more. But are we kinder, less violent, less selfish, less covetous (wanting what other folks have)? I doubt it.

My father once observed that it wasn't that scientists hadn't answered all our questions, it was that they hadn't answered them *yet*. I'd be willing to bet that this is what you were led to believe in school. Maybe nobody has said it that bluntly, but you have been taught by implication that you don't need superstitions like religion, because you have modern science, and modern science can solve all your problems.

But there is one huge problem. No matter how much you learn with your big fancy brain, you are still a physical animal. You still have to find food, mates, and safety. You still have aggression and greed built into your animal self. And no amount of science can change that. Your animal nature is one of the principal things I talk about in this book.

Seduced by progress:

Why do we care if God exists? We care because we have a built-in sense of the holy—beauty, goodness, and truth. But we also care because if there is no God, and our animal natures determine how we behave, there are some awful consequences. History provides us with examples.

I lived most of my life during the terrible twentieth century. Many appalling things happened during the century of my youth: the World Wars, the Holocaust, Viet Nam, Cambodia, Ruanda, the AIDS epidemic, and so forth. We did manage not to blow the world up with the atom bomb, but otherwise we were not getting better and better.

In the twentieth century we believed in "progress." But the twentieth century notion of progress was, at its core, a notion of turning human beings into gods. Someone would figure out how to keep us alive forever, and we would learn how to do away with bad behavior. It is the stuff of science fiction, isn't it? But bad things have continued to happen and the fundamental philosophy continues to this day.

The web of life

This book is based on the fact that we are animals. Any idea of inevitable progress overlooks our unavoidable "creature-ness." Yes, we are fancy, smart, creative animals, but we are related in all but the tiniest ways from the fellow inhabitants of our tiny planet. And because of gene-mapping, we in the twenty first century notice can how intimately connected we are to all other life-forms on Earth as well.

I refer to dogs in the title because although dogs share their lives with us, they do not know they will die. Humans do. And fear of death ignites religious ideas. Always. Someone has said that fear of death is the beginning of wisdom. But every new generation adds new wisdom to religion, because every generation learns new facts about life and death.

Chapter One

The Human Animal

Humans have animal needs and behaviors.

Living with a dog:

When I was fifty years old I acquired my first and only dog. Esther was a shepherd-collie mix, six months old when she escaped from my cousin during a visit to our cottage. I had fallen in love with Esther during the brief time my cousin was with us. Esther was polite, intelligent and obviously sweet, but after she was returned to me I realized that I knew nothing at all about living with a dog. In subsequent years I learned about puppy chewing behavior, housebreaking, cleaning up during walks (I didn't) and not soiling the neighbors' yards (she did). And there were many heart-rending lessons as Esther's health got worse at the end of her life. We struggled to get along, Esther and I, for the nearly twelve years she was with me, and when she finally died I couldn't believe how sad I was.

Until Esther came into my life I don't think I ever really felt like a member of the animal kingdom. Yes, we had cats (lots of cats), but my husband was the cat-guy. Cats were too different, too "other." I never felt much affection for them. And even horses, during the brief summer I was forced to take riding lessons, scared me.

We are animals:

Living with Esther reminded me that we are animals. We eat, breathe, eliminate waste, and have sexual feelings, just as all animals do. Our DNA differs from all other life forms (even vegetables) by only a tiny amount. So before we talk about God, we need to talk more about ourselves as animals.

When I was a girl I was taught that animals don't think, they operate out of instinct. But it was apparent to me that Esther could think. Esther understood my language ("Shall we go for a walk, Esther?") and my emotions (if I was upset she would lay her head in my lap) and my instructions. ("Esther, stay off the couch.") Apparently she understood "what" even if she didn't understand "why." So I have no patience with skeptics who say that animals don't think.

Why is this important? Because no matter how holy we try to be, we always have our animal selves to contend with. But maybe that is a good thing. We observe how clever and sensitive many animals are. For example, birds can respond to music. I once entertained a sparrow, who was sitting outside my open window, with a recording of a string quartet. The sparrow would sing its sparrow song while the recording played Mozart. When I stopped the record, the bird would stop singing. In a similar way I once watched a hawk hover outside an open church window while a soloist sang. The hawk flew away as soon as the singer was finished. So I have not a doubt in the world that birds appreciate musical sounds. And birds, butterflies and bees apparently have an aesthetic sense of color, which pulls them to brightly colored mates and brightly colored flowers. Furthermore, we know that whales and dolphins can communicate in ways that suggest thinking—with dolphins, even, in ways that suggest joking. So the idea that non-human creatures only operate out of instinct is apparently wrong.

Our animal natures also provide us with fundamental survival skills. I love watching the squirrels greedily collect nuts and bury them for the winter. Humans also need to be "greedy"—to care for their physical bodies— in order to survive. But unfortunately we also tend to become covetous and arrogant. We aren't just storing up nuts for hard times, we are building up our self-esteem by having the biggest possible pile of nuts. And then our self-esteem makes us proud of ourselves, so we strut around and become bossy and think we're better than everybody else.

Another animal trait leads to human evil. Animals need to be aggressive, not only to protect themselves from harm but also to acquire desirable mates, and they often fight ferociously to protect their territory.

We can easily see that trait in ourselves as well. Fighting is part of our animal nature, and territorial aggression has been a significant aspect of human sinfulness. Our abstract reasoning provides excuses and weapons. We call it "war."

Talented animals:

Years ago, when we had lots of cats, they sometimes did something that made me laugh. A cat would sit in front of a blank wall and stare at it. Intently. Whatever it was looking at was hypnotizing. (If you are familiar with Kliban cartoons you will remember several drawings of cats staring at walls.) I would say to my husband, "She thinks she sees something," as though this was additional proof of how silly cats were. But in recent years I have come to wonder if, in fact, our cats were seeing something that we couldn't see. Because how do we know what other animals can see? Or, for that matter, how do we know what other animals can hear? We know that dogs seem to go crazy over high pitched sounds that we can't hear. And we believe that dolphins and whales communicate with sounds outside of our normal hearing range.

It is, I suppose, lucky that our seeing and hearing are limited. If we could truly see and hear everything, we would be overwhelmed. Let me tease your imagination here. Suppose you could see radio waves, and whatever other electronic waves make our TVs and computers and automatic clocks work. In your room you could have a TV, a radio, a cordless clock and a wireless computer operating at the same time, all tuned into different wave-lengths. I wonder what that would look like. A great confusing cloud of electronic waves? And then, if you add the CO_2 you have just exhaled, and the vapors given off by your synthetic clothes and furniture covers, the air around you would no longer look transparent and empty. Would it?

Every living thing—plants, bacteria, insects, etc.—interacts with a jungle of invisible substances and forces, and our feeble animal senses probably only experience a small number of these. But certain hyper-sensitive people apparently have experiences that are unavailable to the rest of us. For example, I have known individuals who said they could see "auras," circles of colored energy surrounding human heads. While this has been ridiculed by many skeptics, it would explain the "halos" in classical paintings of holy persons. We will talk later about intuition and other kinds of paranormal experiences. These are experiences outside of our ordinary human-animal abilities. But the fact that they are not part of our everyday lives doesn't mean they are not "real."

What does all of this have to do with our basic questions: Does God exist? and Why do we care? These examples should cause us to rethink our conclusion that if something isn't experienced by our senses, it isn't real. It is "supernatural." Outside of nature. We usually think of religious experiences as supernatural. They can't be experimented with nor experienced by our senses. So because we can't see, hear, taste, smell or feel "God" we conclude there is no such "thing." But, as scientists are often the first to tell us, the more we think we know, the more mysterious Reality (capital R) seems to be. And I am arguing here, and will illustrate in other chapters, we have actual hints of what Shakespeare said were "more things in heaven and earth than are dreamed of in (our) little philosophy."

The complicated human animal:

We assume that dogs and other animals can't believe in God because their brains are not complex enough to have religious ideas and experiences. But human brains are different from dogs and other animals. You have probably seen human skulls in museums with large bony areas above the eye sockets. These would have contained "frontal cortexes"—areas of brain tissue which even advanced animals don't have. Apparently this allows our minds to hold many ideas at the same time. We call this "abstract thinking."

Scientists first studied this ability when prehistoric drawings in French caves were discovered several centuries ago. Cave people apparently had brains developed enough to produce complex thoughts. They painted pictures of animals on their cave walls and, it seems, had primitive religions. We assume they began to wonder where they came from and what meaning their lives had. They "imagined" (an apparently unique human ability) an invisible world which they could portray in pictures.

Perhaps these early humans came up with the idea of super-humans called "gods." We don't know for sure. But think about it. The idea of a super-human creature called a god required imagination and story-telling ability. Can other animals do this? Not that we know of. And here is where humans took a gigantic leap away from their animal ancestors.

Summary:

Humans are animals, first and foremost, and we can't understand ourselves without first taking into account our animal nature. Our animal nature still causes us aggressively to defend ourselves, greedily acquire food, and cause harm to others in our search for mates. But the development of a fancy brain also allows us to remember the past and imagine ourselves into the future.

Chapter Two

When Science is not Scientific

Familiar ideas help us to feel safe in a dangerous world.

Why have we gotten stuck in a non-religious view of existence? And why are religious ideas ridiculed by so many smart people in our lives? Maybe it is because our animal selves are available to be studied by science. But scientists can only study physical existence. And they assume that existence is purely physical. They test the answers to all questions "scientifically" with experiments. (Or with mathematical equations, which are a kind of experiment.) No possible experiment, no legitimate question.

But what's wrong with that? I love science. I am alive because of medical science. I am creating this book on my wonderful Mac-Book, and as far as I can tell, Google will find an answer to any question I can come up with. I am a huge fan of scientific inventions like microwaves and cell phones. I am in awe of the gene-mappers. Science is wonderful beyond anything we could have imagined fifty years ago.

BUT... because scientists only answer questions about our physical existence, they tend to assume that those are the only questions that are worth asking. Therefore if you ask a social scientist what "goodness" means, you will get a social science answer: goodness is behavior that helps us to get along together. If you ask what "beauty" is, you may be told that beauty is whatever any culture thinks it is—there is no such thing as absolute beauty.

Scientism:

I had a scientific upbringing. My parents were modern. They believed that the idea of God was a form of wishful thinking for immature people, and good "reality testing" was a sign of maturity. When I became mature I wouldn't need wishful thinking.

And, as if to prove the point, wishful thinking got me nowhere. I wished that I didn't ever have to be sick, and I was sick a lot. I wished that tornados and floods and wars would never happen, but they all did. If God existed, then God was either mean, or God was helpless, as I could notice in the newspaper every evening.

Then there was school. My history books had a lot of negative things to say about religion: the Crusades, endless religious wars, witch-hunts, and the Catholic Church, which apparently was a bastion of superstition and persecution. My science classes also had a lot of negative things to say about superstition and belief in magic, which were the sources of much evil.

Of course, we never used the word "evil." We studied human beings in the same way that we studied frogs— as a set of physical functions to be taken apart and analyzed. We learned about how species, ourselves included, evolved. We learned about natural selection. If something was written in a textbook, we learned to accept it as True and give it back as an answer to a test.

More than fifty years ago, I learned the following "facts":
1. The Universe had no beginning and will always exist.
2. Water exists only on our earth.
3. The continents were never part of a planetary jigsaw puzzle.
4. We humans are alone in the universe
5. The smallest unit of matter is the electron.
6. Matter can be neither created nor destroyed.
7. We need to beware of "magical thinking" and other non-scientific delusions.

Almost nothing on that list can be proven experimentally. It is a list of guesses. And almost nothing on that list is still believed!. So an important discovery I have made in my long life is that science is not necessarily scientific. Using science to disprove larger ideas about Reality (capital "R") as that list does, is at best arrogant and at worst wrong.

Should we park our scientific brains at the door? No. The wonderful thing about science right now is that so many amazing doors have been pushed ajar that scientists are now using the word "maybe." It is now possible to be deeply religious and creatively scientific at the same time.

Core beliefs:

Why do so many scientific ideas get stuck in the past? We resist new ideas because we do not grow up with empty minds. It is why new ideas are so often ridiculed? Somewhere in the process of growing up we pick up the ideas of the people around us: our parents, our teachers, the TV, our friends, etc.

Many ideas we grew up with turn out to be dangerous. When I was a girl, the idea that cigarettes could make you sick was considered a way to spoil our fun. My parents smoked cigarettes, so obviously it was okay. We were not aware that we were copying their ideas: we labeled them as "common sense." The idea that cigarettes won't hurt you was a core belief among people who smoked.

Here is a more serious (that wasn't serious?) example. We were taught that we are alone in the universe and life has no purpose? Is there scientific evidence for that idea? As I pointed out, scientists are just guessing. It is a core belief.

Here are some other examples of core beliefs:

Do you believe that the only things that are "real" are matter and energy? The smart guys are just guessing about that as well, and I will have more to say about it in the Epilogue.

Do you believe that there is a God who revealed a purpose to us? That is also a core belief which can't be proved scientifically?

Do you believe that if you kill the Unbelievers, you will be rewarded in Heaven. That, sad to say, is another core belief in several parts of the world.

Common sense:

Humans have always held core beliefs that later proved to be false. Once upon a time people believed that the Earth was flat. It's just common sense, isn't it? If the Earth were round, people in South America would fall off. I can remember struggling with that idea when I was a child, and some irrational place in my brain still finds the idea of a round Earth to be ridiculous. Even the idea of gravity seems contrary to common sense; I have an image of up-side-down South Americans, clinging to the Earth by their feet, held on by some force in the same way that iron filings cling to magnets.

My mother used to joke that radios weren't possible. Is it common sense that sounds could be the same everywhere, so that we could listen to Jack Benny on the radio in Michigan and at the same time my cousins could listen to him in Chicago? No? So radios are impossible, right?

Well, we were all experiencing radios in the same way at the same time, so obviously they were "real," however irrational that seemed.

We all use common sense. Mostly common sense refers to what we experience, what the people around us believe, and in particular, what we are taught in school. Common sense creates an aura of truth around what we are willing to believe. We accept ideas of reality only if they fit within the closed boundaries of our common sense. *Common sense says that something is real if we can experience it with our senses and test it scientifically, preferably with a control sample.* (We heard Jack Benny in Ann Arbor and our control sample heard him in Chicago.) If we can't test it scientifically, we should not assume it is real.

The trouble is, science can only explore experiences that can be repeated and, preferably, measured. (Jack Benny was on the radio every Sunday night, and the radio wave lengths could be measured.) One of-a-kind occurrences are dismissed as "anecdotal," which means evidence based on casual observation, rather than scientific evidence. But you will notice that much of science and medicine is already based on anecdotal evidence. "On a scale of one to ten, how bad is your pain?" the doctor asks you. "Are you feeling better? Where does it hurt?" Questions like that require anecdotal answers.

I will talk from now on about anecdotal ideas. But that, I think you will see, doesn't mean that they are not true. Even scientists these days talk about the "receding horizon of knowledge." In other words, even scientists are aware that the more we know, the more we realize we don't know.

Summary:

It is no longer unscientific to look with wonder on the many unexplained aspects of Reality that surround us. The best stance seems to be one of open-mindedness, because many things that used to seem impossible now appear to be at least worth studying. What does all this have to do with our search for God? It suggests that, as the psychologist William James once wrote, "We are probably separated from other realities by the thinnest of veils." It is those "thin veils" I will talk about in the rest of this book.

Chapter Three

Creatures With Souls

Humans are "hard-wired" for God.

Okay. So far I've danced around the main subject. Does God exist? And why do we care? But of course, that really is only one subject. *The main subject is: How do we know that God exists?* If that question is answered, the second one answers itself, doesn't it? If you knew beyond the shadow of a doubt that God, as you learned about God in church, actually exists, exactly as you have been told, then you'd be the biggest fool imaginable not to care.

It goes without saying that no matter how long and passionately I talked about God to my dog Esther, she wouldn't get it. So I need to begin this chapter by considering ourselves, human animals, as differing from our fellow animals on Earth in this fundamental way: our fancy brains allow us to have "spiritual" experiences that are unavailable to lower animals. What does that mean? It means that because we have some trace of spirituality in ourselves, we can experience a spiritual entity whom we call "God." (If we were just "things," as my granddaughter was taught in school, then no doubt we invented religion to make ourselves feel better.)

The brain is not a computer:

Let's begin by noticing that the brain is more complicated than any possible computer can ever be. Recently an inventor announced confidently that he would produce a computer that could "think" in every way that people think. "This computer will answer any question that a person can ask, and will in every other way be better than a human mind," he asserted. But however smart computers may be, they don't have unique memories, and no computer can grieve, no computer can laugh, no computer can dream. Computers can only solve problems fed to them by humans. "Garbage in, garbage out," as the familiar joke has it.

But if our brains are not computers, what are they? Are they merely chemical-electrical factories that produce thoughts? No brain, no thoughts? That seems to be common sense. But what are "thoughts"? What is happening when you "think"?

Your brain produces electricity when you think. We know that much. An electro-encephalogram (EEG) will even show what kind of thinking you're doing: problem solving, or fanaticizing, or dreaming. Your brain waves will be different for each activity. Or a brain scanner (MRI) will show where blood flow is concentrated in your head. But the EEG and the MRI will only tell you about the factory (brain function), not the actual product (thoughts).

Why does it matter? Because our minds turn out to be enormously more complicated than simple brain waves would indicate. We know that when someone's brain is injured, by a stroke for instance, the non-injured part of the brain can gradually take over the functioning of the damaged part. The mind seems to discover a route for thoughts, even when the brain is partially functioning.

Our layered minds:

Thoughts themselves are complex. We do not have one thought at a time, and then string our thoughts together like little beads. That's not how our minds work. Our minds contain layers of thoughts, all at once. At the same time that I am writing this sentence, I am vaguely aware of being hungry, of missing my dad, and of a backache. Yes, all at the same time. I can pull a thought into the foreground—become more aware of it—but the others are still present. When I drive a car, I notice that I can pay attention to traffic, eat my hamburger, and talk to my friend, all at the same time.

And that's just my conscious mind. Below its surface is an ocean of potential thoughts and feelings, which remain hidden, out of awareness.

These underneath-layers of our minds are called "the unconscious." For years this idea was ridiculed, but these days we can examine the unconscious by studying brain waves.

The unconscious mind is odd in a number of ways. For example, the unconscious mind mostly contains images, not words. Can you think without words? Of course. Try this simple experiment. Look out the window at a tree. Now, describe the tree to yourself in words. Notice how difficult it is; how your mind shifts gears. Your initial experience of the tree had no words connected to it. And, indeed, much "thinking" has no words.

Are you getting ready to argue that advanced computers can do most of those things? Well…yes…but read on.

Dreaming

We also think without words in our dreams. Dreams, with their bizarre images, are little night-windows into our unconscious minds. It often feels as though our dreams make no sense. In fact, critics of dream-analysis have sometimes called dreaming "the garbage container for our waking lives." They claim that we dump unwelcome ideas and experiences into our dreams to be rid of them in some way. And it is true that if you eat too many pickles and spicy foods before you go to bed, your stomach may give you a garbage-filled dream.

However most of our dreams are not garbage at all. They are odd stories, filled with puzzling characters and events. And usually we dream in code, using symbols and other mysterious images. But that does not mean that a dream has no meaning.

Let me share a dream that was once told to me:

> The dreamer was lost in Ann Arbor, finding himself in the Arcade, which is a covered walkway with openings at each end, then on Liberty Street, and finally at the corner of State Street and South University. It made no sense. Nothing was happening. He was just there.

When he later thought about the locations themselves, meaning appeared. The Arcade was open-ended. The word "liberty" had great meaning in his life at that time. He also realized that at the corner of State Street and South University were the Law School and the Union. All important themes—codes—with larger meanings in his waking life.

Why do we dream in code? Apparently we dream in code in order to deal with ideas that are too scary, sad or threatening to think about when we are awake. We have repressed these ideas. We don't know we're doing it; thus the word "unconscious." But at night, when we're dreaming, this repressed material leaks into our sleeping minds in unthreatening ways. The codes make puzzles out of ideas that would be too sad or scary to look at in the light of day.

Notice how clever and complex the codes were in the dream I described. They didn't say to the dreamer, "Look, you idiot, get out of the marriage that imprisons you," nor did they say, "Talk to a lawyer." But the messages were there if he was ready to deal with them. Or they would remain hidden if he was not.

Dreams are products of our physical lives: our emotions, our desires, our imaginations—all aspects of life that computers can never share with us.

Summary:

Our brains are infinitely more complicated than any computer could be, as we discover when we explore the multiple layers of our thinking process.

Chapter Four

Communicating with God

Our minds are not confined by time and space.

I am taking it for granted that human minds are better than computers, which can only problem-solve. Human minds also differ from the minds of lower animals, which (as far as we know) can only process one idea at a time. (Yes, I have noticed cats and dogs dreaming, but we don't know what those dreams are about.) We refer to ourselves as "spiritual creatures" because our conscious and unconscious thoughts seem to be infinitely creative. as we notice in our subtle and inventive ability to dream.

But what about when we are awake? Is what we call "prayer" merely a form of day dreaming, or is it some sort of communication? Can we actually communicate with God when we are awake? Most religious people believe that we can. So in order to understand how that might work, let's examine one more aspect of our amazing unconscious

Sarah R. Taggart

minds.

Here is a true story:

A few years ago I wrote an essay about a big red "Oxford Book of English Verse," that I was given for my eleventh birthday. I learned that one of my best friends, Mary Lea Bird, had the same book, and we decided to get together on successive Saturdays to have picnics and share poetry. It was a very special time—we took our books and our lunches into the crook of a big willow tree near my Ann Arbor home and fell in love with Wordsworth and Shelley and Keats.

Nothing came of my recent essay—it was tucked away in my computer—but several days after I wrote it I had a phone call from a small town in southwest Michigan. A woman's voice asked, "Were you once Sarah Riggs?" When I said I was, the voice said, "This is Mary Lea Bird. For some reason your name just popped into my mind." I nearly dropped the phone. I hadn't heard from or about Mary Lea Bird in more than fifty years!

The collective unconscious:

Early in the twentieth century a famous psychologist, Carl Jung, came up with a new idea of how our minds work. He called this ability of our minds, "the collective unconscious." He was puzzled by the existence of identical ideas that are shared by people and cultures which have no contact with each other. He concluded that the unconscious minds of all humans are embedded with ideas and images that are independent of experience—especially religious ideas and images—and that minds can communicate with each other, even when they are far apart. That, apparently, was what happened in my contact with Mary Lea Bird.

Some examples can be found in stories about extra-sensory perception, reincarnation, savantism, and artistic talent—impossible experiences which nonetheless actually happen. Jung called this odd ability, "the collective unconscious," but others have suggested that it may include the expression of God's "thoughts" in our world of time and space.

Experiencing the impossible:

Perhaps our minds connect with God through the collective unconscious.

We used to joke about "déjà vu" when we felt that that something new was oddly familiar. But, gradually, evidence has accumulated that this may not be a mere superstition. It may even be a lost memory from another life, as the following story illustrates. How weird is that? If so, then our minds truly are more than chemicals and electricity. Distortions of time and space may exist in other ways than in science fiction.

Here is a true story:

A University of Virginia medical school professor, the late Ian Stevenson, spent nearly forty years examining the possibility of reincarnation. This means, as I'm sure you know, the reappearance of a dead person's personality in a new body. Over a forty-year period, Stevenson compiled careful records of more than 1000 cases of apparent reincarnation.

Of course, if reincarnation were true, it would mean that not only is the mind not a product of the brain, *the mind apparently has an independent existence*, as we are suggesting in this chapter. It didn't seem likely.

Tom Shroder, a former Washington Post reporter, had already considered a number of reincarnation studies, including the famous Brian Weiss "past lives" explorations under hypnosis (Weiss, *Many Lives, Many Masters*, Simon and Schuster 1988). Shroder had concluded that serious scientists could come up with explanations other than reincarnation. However, before dismissing reincarnation entirely, he was urged to talk with Ian Stevenson. Schroder decided to do an in-depth interview to see if Stevenson, perhaps, had evidence worth taking seriously. But he fully expected to debunk Stevenson's conclusions, as he and others had debunked Weiss's.

After initial hesitation, Stevenson invited Shroder to accompany him on what might be his last research journey (he was then seventy nine years old) to India and Lebanon. He explained to Shroder that his research subjects had been very small children who reported to their parents that they had different names in previous lives, and came from other families.

Stevenson believed that this phenomenon occurs everywhere, but in India and Lebanon, reincarnation was part of the accepted belief system, so the parents took their children's stories seriously. However, the "recall" had to occur in the earliest possible years of the child's life, and usually involved a traumatic event that caused the previous life to be snuffed out—in an auto accident, for example. By the time a child was age five or so, too many events in the present life had intruded and the memories faded. "Maybe remembering is a defect," Stevenson said. "Maybe we're supposed to forget."

Stevenson had followed up many cases for more than forty years, and had several old cases to introduce to Shroder on their trip together. Shroder's amazing book (*Old Lives, Old Souls*, Fireside 1999), which recounts his travels with Stevenson, contains dozens of case histories, as well as some astonishing photographs. In the end, Shroder was persuaded that no other explanation made sense, though he agreed with Stevenson in saying that he had no idea how reincarnation would work. Goodbye to traditional notions of mind-body connections.

The Real World:

The Real World is the world of chemistry and physics—material cause and effect—only.

Ian Stevenson was remarkably persistent and lucky in finding a professional world which did not discount his life work as being "unscientific." Unfortunately, conventional science exists within what is called a "closed system." That is, most scientists assume that all human experience originates in the Real World. Puzzling occurrences like reincarnation have traditionally been discounted by scientists, because they cannot occur in the Real World.

Fortunately there is a sub-specialty of psychology called "parapsychology," which studies events that seem to occur outside of the traditional "closed system" of experience. *Parapsychology uses terms like extrasensory perception, pre-cognition, and psycho-kinesis, and has frequently been ridiculed, even though many of its experiments have been carefully designed and scientifically controlled* (see Broughton, *Parapsychology: The Controversial Science*, Ballantine 1991). The Parapsychology Association has been a member of the American Association for the Advancement of Science, but I'll bet a million dollars that most readers have never heard it. Why? Because parapsychology is dismissed as being outside the Real World.

"It isn't true, because it can't be true."

Savants:

In the Real World, each "thing" seems to be a local (separate) entity. But scientist are now considering a seemingly impossible idea. It begins to look like *everything in our world is connected to everything else. Actually.*

Physically. There are no "local" objects or events. (I will explain this more fully in the Epilogue.) So I want to talk now about several odd example of "non-locality"

We have an example of apparently non-local minds in individuals referred to as "savants." *Savants know things that they have no way to know—they seem to pull knowledge out of thin air* .

Here is another true story:

On the CBS program, "Sixty Minutes" (June 25, 2006), viewers were introduced to a charming little ten year old named Rex Lewis-Clack. Rex was both retarded and blind from birth. He couldn't dress himself, and got lost in his very small apartment. But he was a musical prodigy. From his earliest years he had an amazing ear for music, which began when his parents gave him a little keyboard for his second birthday. The TV viewer sees a home-movie of this toddler putting his hands on the magic keyboard. Almost immediately he responded emotionally to the sounds he was creating. By the time he was four he could immediately repeat almost any musical composition he heard. Now, at the age of ten, he was giving public concerts, and his teacher foresaw a possible adult career for him.

Musical geniuses like Rex are usually blind, and are frequently autistic. The CBS show took viewers to a "home" for autistic musicians in England, where their talents could be honed and their severe physical needs met. "There is," the reporter, Leslie Stahl, noted sadly, "no such institution in the USA." But why blindness, retardation, and musical genius occur together is a great mystery. No theories of how the mind works can account for it.

Autistic savants are not solely geniuses in the musical realm. Sometimes they seem to be mathematical geniuses instead. If you saw the movie, "The Rain Man," starring Dustin Hoffman, you encountered another example of an autistic savant—someone who could perform seemingly impossible feats of mathematical memory. Based on a true story, the movie tells about a retarded man who could tell the day of the week—Monday, Tuesday, Wednesday, etc.—of any date in history. He could pull the day of the week out of the air in an instant. This sort of numbers-feat is fairly common among mathematical savants, some of whom can also list prime numbers into the many thousands of digits. The big question is, how do savants do it?

Let's invent a myth:

> Deep in the Australian bush lives a tribe of Aboriginal people who have never encountered contemporary Australians, except when an occasional trekker hikes past their village. One day a child finds a small black box lying in the desert and takes it home. As children do, he starts poking and pushing the little things that stick out, and all of a sudden

the little black box starts to make sounds.

He runs to his parents with the box and says, "Look! The box sings."

Pretty soon all the villagers gather around to listen to the singing box. But after awhile the child pokes it again and the singing stops.

"You killed the box," complains a villager.

But a wise elder notices what the child poked, and tries poking it himself. The box starts to sing again.

The village chief is a sensible man. "There is a bird in the box," he explains. "We should liberate the bird."

So the people take the box apart, and lo! there is no bird.

And after that, the box is angry and sings no more.

The box, as you have realized, is a battery-powered radio, left by accident by one of the trekkers. Did something alive inside the box create the sounds? No. The explanation turns out to be even more mysterious. Something out of the air created the sounds. Radio waves.

Maybe our minds are "radios." This is not the newest idea in the world. There is a wonderful gospel song, "Turn Your Radio On," that you may be familiar with. Is it possible that savant minds are like the little black box in my Australia story? More like "receivers" than "manufacturers"? Maybe ordinary brains are filters, and savant brains lack adequate filters.

But whatever explains it, something strange is going on with the startling talents of savants. It seems obvious that physical brains cannot by themselves be responsible.

The Arts:

We communicate our experience of the collective unconscious through the Arts: poetry, music, painting, drama, etc.

Here's a question for you. Do you have an artistic talent of some sort? Maybe you are an artist or a musician. Maybe you like to act or to design gardens. If so, you could be said to be a "savant" in another sense.

I myself come from an artistic family. My sister was painting wonderful pictures while she was still in grade school. Had someone taught her to do this? No. Her unconscious mind compelled her to create pictures, and a lifetime later she is still at it. My youngest son could remember melodies after hearing them only once by the time he was four, and has always had "perfect pitch." Even though he studied to be a chemist, his musical aptitude remained the driving force of his psyche, and his adult vocation is now music education.

We refer to these abilities as "talents," but I believe they are entirely mysterious. I think they are windows into the collective unconscious. This is what distinguishes serious Art (capital "A") from commercial art.

The Arts call up material from the Collective Unconscious (I will use capital letters, because I think we are encountering the Divine here), clothes it in images (thus the word "imagination") and transmits it to the conscious mind of the artist. Who then conveys it to the rest of us.

Worship experiences also can reflect the Collective Unconscious. Pastors note times when the Holy Spirit seemed especially present at a service: "Everyone in the congregation seemed caught up in the sermon and the music," one of them said to me once. Perhaps our spiritual natures become connected with each other and with the Universal Mind during worship.

Summary:

Scientists have taught us that the only things that are "real" are happenings or things that are available to be tested. The Real World is the closed world of science. But odd experiences like apparent reincarnation, the impossible feats of savants, and the seemingly inexplicable talents of serious Artists, suggest the existence of invisible worlds entirely outside "the Real World."

Chapter Five

The Devil In The Details

Most of God's purposes are hidden from us.

We have been talking about how our unconscious minds apparently connect us to a spiritual consciousness that we refer to as "God." But that ability alone does not help us to understand who God is. And the objection that our critics immediately offer is "if God is so wonderful, why do bad things happen to good people?" So before we go further, let's admit that this question is hard to answer.

I wish I could talk about God as a good papa who didn't let bad things happen at all—God as Santa Claus. But from the beginning of the human adventure, the idea of punishment has always been connected to ideas about the gods.

Gods are believed to require certain behaviors of humans—these are the "rules" of all religions. And disobedience (sin) is believed to be followed by punishment.

These days we don't think of ourselves as "disobeying God." We obey our laws. We are kind to our children. We don't tell lies (mostly). So what on earth did we do to deserve all this punishment? If there is such a thing as God, isn't God overdoing it? Why didn't God save the Jews during the Holocaust? Why did God let the Hutus murder the Tutsis in Ruanda? Why did God let the twin towers be destroyed?

Our sinful natures:

Unfortunately, human animals didn't leave their primitive needs and behaviors behind when they developed fancy brains. And their fancy brains made things worse. Do we still compete for mates, territory and power, just as our jungle relatives do? Look around. Read the newspapers. The problem begins with our animal aggressiveness and need for food, safety, and sex, but once we begin to puff ourselves up and make excuses for our behavior, it begins to be "sin."

Why do we say that the human animal "sins," yet, for example, our cats could tease and torture mice and we don't call that sin? Or my dog Esther could try to bite the mailman without being guilty of a sin. The answer is that we don't consider something a "sin" if the creature "doesn't know any better." Unfortunately, humans do know better, and too often we do it anyway.

Sin is an unpleasant idea, and in the twenty first century we spend a lot of time ridiculing it. Maybe, as the smart guys say, human progress will eliminate the primitive idea of sin. "The idea of sin," they tell us, "is just a way to scare us into being religious. Education and modern civilization will enable us to do away with such primitive ideas."

But have they? Inevitably we continue to contend with our animal natures, and as a consequence, sin and evil refuse to go away. Civilization merely makes sin and evil more organized and efficient. Americans in the twenty first century thought that "shock and awe"—the astonishing bombing of civilians in Iraq—was somehow justified by our advanced civilization. When we observe these ghastly outcomes on our TV's every night, we wonder why we keep on behaving so badly? Could it be that we keep on behaving badly because we are still animals? Apparently, even though we invented computers and TV's, we have not eliminated all the self protective behaviors that we inherited from our animal forebears.

God's self-imposed limits:

There is a familiar saying that you may have heard: *"If God is great, He is not good; if God is good, He is not great."* The saying means that an all-powerful God could prevent bad things from happening, but because bad things do happen, one should conclude that God is not all powerful.

But we can begin to understand God's problems with us earthly creatures by thinking about our own everyday experiences. For example, my dog Esther could not understand why I wouldn't let her pee in the house or sleep on the couch. In the same way, my two year old son could not understand why I made him sit up straight at the dinner table and eat with a fork. Sitting on the floor and eating with his hands must have seemed so much more sensible to his two year old mind. But of course, my two year old son was eventually going to grow up, and table manners would eventually be important, even if his two year old mind couldn't understand that. And my dog Esther was going to have to live in a clean house with irrational humans, even if her doggy brain may have thought that to be unnecessary.

Just as we don't try to explain adult reasoning to a two year old, we assume that God can't explain the workings of the universe to his limited creatures.

The Inscrutable God:

In the Biblical story of Job, we find a dramatic explanation of God's seemingly irrational behavior. This fictional story is about a good man's incredible bad fortune and his anger at God for punishing him when he didn't do anything wrong. His friends are unable to discover anything Job did to deserve all the bad things that happened to him. However, Job finally hears a mysterious Voice Out of a Whirlwind (God) saying: "Where were you when I laid the foundations of the earth?" (Job 38:4)

What does that mean? It means that God's purposes—God's rules—are as hard for humans to understand as are the rules of parents in refusing to let small children sit on the floor and eat with their hands. Though the process may be messy at first, their parents say that "we know best." We assume it is the same with God.

Most of God's purposes are hidden from us because of our physical limitations—our animal selves. Unavoidably. How could it be otherwise? Maybe God can interfere once in awhile (we call them "miracles") but mostly the web of life spins on in its mysterious way. So the truthful answer to the "theodicy" question (the study of good and evil) is that we aren't able to know God's ultimate purposes.

This sounds like "rationalizing"—like making up a reason to support an unreasonable conclusion. But religion's critics aren't reasonable either. They describe the outcome of the Big Bang, including the astonishing laws of nature, as resulting from a tiny, meaningless speck of who-knows-what. Does that explanation make sense? For myself, I am content to say that I don't know why evil exists. But I experience God in so many positive ways that I accept that God knows what God is doing.

The creation of opposites:

We do know one thing about God's self-imposed limits, because something amazing happened at the instant of Creation.

At the instant of the Big Bang, opposites were created.

The Bible tells us that the Creator said, "Let there be light." But in order for there to be "light" there had to be darkness with which it was contrasted. (The Bible uses the word "void," which must mean the absence of light.) And we have pictures!! Out of the left-over sky from the moment of the Big Bang, astronomers have photographs of an astonishingly beautiful explosion of colors—of brilliant light. Whatever else was going on at the instant of Creation, it surely did involve "light."

So we can notice one central reason that God seems to us not to be all-powerful. It happened at the moment of the Big Bang, when the physical universe came into existence. The Voice Out of the Whirlwind's explanation to Job was majestic and overwhelming, but there is actually is a more down-to-earth explanation for the existence of good and evil in the world.

Think about it. How would you understand light if you had never experienced darkness? How would you know that something was "good" if you had never experienced anything "bad"? How would you know what "soft" meant if you had never experienced anything "hard"? These are "paradoxes." *"Paradox" means anything that contains its opposite. We live in a "paradoxical" cosmos.*

We have knowledge of both good and evil, because we are physical creatures, living in a paradoxical universe. Good and evil are linked-together opposites. We cannot understand one without the other, because they are "paradoxically" joined.

In contrast to all other animals, we spend our lives choosing between the opposites of good and evil.

Becoming more God-like:

You realize, if you have read this far, that I have been avoiding the word "evolution." This word is so toxic, so poisoned with personal opinion and misinformation, that I wish I could just skip it altogether. But alas, no. So let's examine the idea of evolution with our two questions in mind: Does God exist? And Why should we care?

Let's re-word those questions: Where did we come from? And is there any purpose to our existence? Let's think about the evolution of human beings, which you learn about in school and which I'm taking for granted here.

There are three ideas about evolution:

First idea: Maybe evolution happened "by chance"—there was no "reason" for it. (The scientific explanation).

Second idea: Maybe it didn't happen at all, and we magically appeared in the world just as we are now. (The Biblical Fundamentalist explanation).

Or, third idea: Maybe evolution is always in the direction of more complexity and greater consciousness. (The wonderful physicist, Freeman Dyson, said this in a book I admire very much: *Infinite In All Directions*, Harper Collins, 1988). One doesn't have to rely on religion to believe this idea, one has only to look around. We know enough scientifically to notice that we are smarter and more complicated than our nearest relatives, monkeys.

Survival of the fittest:

Apparently God causes animals to become more complicated and intelligent over time.

Why? Our religions suggest that we are to become more God-like—that God wants company. Is that true? We don't know. But we can observe that we "evolve" through what the scientists call "natural selection," which could only occur when life-forms could die, and then be "reborn" better in some better way. So "death" has been associated with "life" from the very beginning.

You undoubtedly learned about natural selection in your biology class. Natural selection means that the best adapted of any life form—not just animals, but plants, fish, bacteria, you name it—will tend to succeed against all odds, and reproduce. This is called "survival of the fittest." How do we know this has happened? Because we find remains of outmoded life-forms on our beaches and driveways and mountainsides. We call these "fossils."

Let's think about survival of the fittest. If survival were beautiful and easy, would creatures evolve? Probably not. Leisure and prosperity are not character building, because fat, lazy (slow) animals will not survive in a world of wolves and bad bacteria . Doesn't life's struggle itself cause natural selection to work? The most clever and brave pass on positive traits to their off-spring, who also become clever and brave. Danger and competition are not necessarily bad things.

As religious people, we are willing to put up with evolution's challenges because we are convinced that life is God's classroom, not God's playground. I'll have more to say about this later.

Why Sex is a Great Thing.

We live in a sexual world. Our sexuality is the source of much—maybe even most—of our energy and creativity.

Animals, birds, plants—you name it—become increasingly seductive and beautiful in order to attract the opposite sex. But think about what a stroke of genius the creation of sexuality was in the first place? After all, if we reproduced by cloning ourselves, we could avoid an awful lot of the messiness involved in attracting mates.

Of all God's bright ideas, sexuality was the brightest. Really. "Male and female, created He them," it says in the Book of Genesis, but we aren't told what God's thinking was. "Male and female" means everything: flowers, fish, birds, insects.

The creation of sexuality seems to be the driving force of evolution; the force that sends birds migrating halfway around the world, and bees into sexy little flowers, and bull elks crashing into each other during mating season. It is the primary force that creates human families, and much of human sin.

It is also the force than creates love.

Sarah R. Taggart

Why Love?

The evolution of love is the central aspect of our animal nature. And we are told that when we learn to love, we learn about God's love.

Humans do not have a corner on love. I recently watched a pair of doves, which had created one of their precarious nests on a window sill near where I was working. They took turns sitting on the nest. As we know, doves mate for life, as do many other birds. Is that love? Who knows? But there is something poignant and familiar about birds that mate for life. I think about a lone cardinal who lost her mate, hanging out alone with other cardinals year after year, as happened in our yard not long ago. And many mammals seem especially loving. Anyone who has owned a dog has experienced this. Anyone who has seen movies of wolves or bears caring for their young realizes that the cubs are tenderly loved. One of the qualities we most admire in dolphins is their seeming affection, not only for each other but for us, whenever we are around them.

Summary:

Human nature differs from animal nature because our evolved brains can make choices in a paradoxical world in which good is contrasted to evil, and therefore to understand the nature of sin. And our struggles to survive allow us to grow our souls.

Chapter Six

The Great Unknowable

Metaphors translate the unknown into the known.

We have talked about how our minds work— about layers of "consciousness" and about how these enable us to have complex thoughts and experiences. Now I want to consider how our minds can imagine the unimaginable.

Human imagination:

You and I both know that we are not "just" animals. I don't know a dog who can write stories, nor a bird who can sing hymns. We are animals, yes, but we are more than animals. In this chapter I want to explore this "more-ness." I want to awaken your science-fiction self— to loosen your imagination and to consider the vast, mysterious arena of the "spiritual."

Let's begin by talking about mystery. I don't mean "fantasy" or "fiction.".

I mean "unknowable." I need to shake us loose from the idea that the "Real" is only what we can actually experience. In this chapter I want to explore a wonderful aspect of humanness that causes us to be enormously different from our animal ancestors—the human imagination.

In these days of scientific explorations, imagination has gotten a bad reputation, but scientists tell us that even on scientific frontiers, most new discoveries begin in the imagination of some clever scientist, who then "dreams up" experiments and theories. So we need to acknowledge that above all, it is our imaginations that make us uniquely human.

Your own imagination probably goes back to your earliest childhood, at least as far back as your make-believe playmates, the tooth fairy, Santa Claus, and the Easter Bunny. You probably used the phrase "I believe" when you thought about these ideas. But all of these were, you eventually learned, "just superstitions." Making the leap, at some point, between believing in Santa Claus and "believing" in God required a distinction between "superstition" (Santa Claus) and "metaphor" (God) that many young people don't know how to make. So "God" gets dismissed as just another superstition.

I'll get to metaphors in a moment, but first let's clarify what a superstition is.

Superstitions:

What is a superstition? *A superstition says if you take an action, something unrelated will happen.* Think of examples from childhood. "Stepping on a crack" will not "break your mother's back." There is no relationship between a crack in the sidewalk and your mother's spine. The two are not related in any way. Tossing salt over your shoulder will not bring you good luck, and getting up out of the wrong side of the bed will not bring you bad luck. And even though one day, when you wore a red shirt to school, you got an A on an exam, wearing that shirt to subsequent exams will not guarantee you A's. There is no relationship between shirts and exam grades.

As I said earlier, once upon a time humans thought that they were surrounded by super-humans they called "gods." These gods were, in most respects, like themselves, only more so. There were lots of them, each one with a different talent and responsibility. If you have read "The Iliad," the Greek tragedies, or the Norse legends, you have encountered these gods. (Or, if you do crossword puzzles, you know that the Norse God of War was "Odon".) We refer to these so-called "gods" as "superstitions."

Before there was science, primitive peoples used superstitions to try to feel safe in their dangerous world. (Noticing how dangerous their worlds were was a price to be paid for their big fancy brains.) When primitive groups had to figure out life's mysteries, they put their newly evolved imaginations to work. They got together and told tales of magic and wonderment. They attempted to make sense out of their short lives by noticing how some activities seemed to cause unrelated things to happen.

If they danced in a particular way, the rains came. If they used a magic talisman, the sick person got well. These were superstitions.

It is true that superstitious ideas live on in many of our religious practices. *It is the task of organized religion to maintain powerful connections to the past.* And so, at some point, some former superstitions have become metaphors, which I will get to in a minute.

Unfortunately, some old superstitious ideas persist, in spite of solid scientific evidence to the contrary. It seems amazing that the lovely Creation stories in the Biblical Book of Genesis, which were, no doubt, told around campfires by the prehistoric Hebrews, are not now understood as "metaphorical." There is no "universal" creation story, not in the Bible and not in the world. In the Old Testament are *two* creation stories, not just one, which have been more or less melded together in the early chapters of the Book of Genesis. It is relatively easy to pry them apart, and to see how two different cultures originally imagined the beginning of the world. These stories were once ancient superstitions. We know that all primitive people everywhere have "creation stories" and no two of them are identical.

I bring this up because Bible "literalists" insist that Bible stories are exactly true; God telling the writers of the Bible exactly what to write. But I am arguing that superstitious stories that get re-told through the ages, such as the Creation stories, usually have meanings greater than the actual events, and that is why the stories are remembered.

It is those "greater meanings" that we refer to as metaphors.

The limits of experience:

One night, when one of my sons was about five years old, he couldn't get to sleep. After asking for the usual glass of water, he finally said in a troubled voice, "Mom, I won't know how to be a grownup."

Oh dear. How should I answer that? What I recall saying was, "When you were three, did you think you would know how to be five? You'll figure it out when the time comes."

But no child knows how to be a grownup. It is such a universal problem that St. Paul even talks about it in the Bible. (I Corinthians 13) And the problem is even bigger.

The problem is, we can't imagine what we can't possibly experience.

If we are deaf from birth, we can't imagine music; deaf people often think of music in terms of vibrations, musical rhythms that they can feel through their feet. Is that "music"? Not really. If we are blind from birth, we can't imagine colors; blind people sometimes imagine colors in terms of taste. But that isn't accurate either.

We are condemned by our physical senses (sight, hearing, taste, touch, smell) to imagine the unknown in terms of the known, just as a blind person imagines colors (the unknown) in terms of taste (the known).

We call these comparisons "metaphors." This is central to everything I will talk about from now on. People tend to be sloppy with the idea of metaphors, but unless you understand it, you might as well stop reading. *If you still wonder if God exists, then the word "metaphor" will be the key to unlocking the mysteries.*

The glorious metaphor:

A metaphor means any comparison between an unknown idea and a known experience.

Metaphors always stand for something else. For example, scientists tell us that the idea of the "electron" is a metaphor. They don't know what electrons "really" look like, they only know how electrons seem to behave. They imagine them to be little dots, or tiny balls, because they know about dots and balls, and the image helps them to draw diagrams. They are imagining the unknown (actual electrons) in terms of the known (little balls). This is a metaphor.

Metaphors can be tiny and poetic ("an easy exam is like a walk in the park") or huge and complex (God created the Universe). Metaphors can be simple—an electron is a little ball— or they can be complex— myths, legends and parables, which we call "extended metaphors."

(My granddaughter once complained, correctly, that comparisons using the word "like" are called "similes." But I am going to use the word "metaphor" to include "similes" and all imaginative comparisons of any kind, and if your English teacher doesn't like it, too bad.)

We use metaphors all the time. *The metaphor allows us to explain experiences, feelings and ideas that plain language would miss.* Here are some common metaphors (from Google). When someone is very upset, we say she is "bouncing off the walls." When an argument becomes very intense, we say it is "a heated debate," and we tell people to "chill out." If an argument seems to be "going nowhere," we say it is "beating a dead horse." When young people like something very much, they say it is "cool". We say that someone "falls" in love.

And so forth.

Summary:

Human imagination clothes the utterly unknowable in the known images that we call "metaphors," including myths, legends and parables. In particular, religion clothes the Great Unknown in metaphors in order to make it available to ourselves as human animals, with our physical limitations.

Chapter Seven

Christian Metaphors

Jesus' was a master of the metaphor

We come now to Jesus of Nazareth. Whatever the literal truth of the Jesus story (I'll get to that) we should all be in awe of his teaching. Above all we should be in awe of Jesus' metaphorical stories. We call them "parables," but basically they are Christian extended metaphors.

Many of Jesus' parables begin with the phrase "The Kingdom of Heaven is like…" Jesus' parables make comparisons between an unknown (the Kingdom of Heaven) and the known (stories about households and farmers and servants). Jesus' stories—his metaphors— are so vivid (and so puzzling) that they have become part of our language and culture. For instance, most of us know the story of "The Prodigal Son," and "The Good Samaritan," even if we don't know a whole lot about Christianity in general.

Jesus' most familiar metaphor is the word he used to describe God:

the metaphor of "Father." We say that God is like a father. Is God really like my father? Well, my father couldn't be everywhere at once (though it sometimes seemed that way) and certainly never created anything more complicated than a funny story. But he was kind, intelligent and loving. Would God at least have those qualities? Probably. Would God be more than that? Undoubtedly.

The Gospels:

Jesus never wrote anything down.

During the brief three years of his public ministry, Jesus and his followers were "on the move," and all of his teaching was in the form of spoken ideas and stories. SO... everything Jesus taught eventually had to be retold through the words and memories of others.

After Jesus was gone, his followers told stories about wonderful and miraculous events that they had witnessed, and various scribes and scholars did write Jesus' stories down so they wouldn't be forgotten. But it is important to remember that *we have many accounts of Jesus' life and teaching—especially the four Gospels of the New Testament, in the Bible.* These are the Gospels of Matthew, Mark, Luke and John. ("Gospel" means "Good News.)

Who were Matthew, Mark, Luke and John? We don't know for sure. They inform us that they were friends of Jesus' disciples. Why did they select certain events and stories? No doubt because those events and stories seemed best to illustrate what they believed Jesus was all about—in other words, *the metaphorical meaning of Jesus' life.* Three of the Gospels tell variations of the same stories, but each Gospel contains stories that are unique to it.

Did the disciples remember some of Jesus' actual words? Probably, just as you and I can remember lines of poetry, or certain things that loved people have said to us. But the word "select" is important. The Gospel writers selected what stories to include.

Were all the stories "true"?

No one knows, and most importantly, no one can ever know. We weren't there.

What really happened?

The Gospel stories are collections of many memories and metaphors, but how do we know what really happened? Let me answer with another story.

I have a vivid memory of my New Testament teacher at Pomona College, Merriman Cunningim, telling the story of the last week of Jesus' life: the donkey ride into Jerusalem on Palm Sunday, the Last Supper, the Betrayal, and the drama of the Passion, Crucifixion and Resurrection.

"Could you imagine a more compelling story?" he asked the hushed class, caught up in the intensity of his narration. "Could you improve on it?"

"But was it true?" someone asked.

"If you had been there, would you forget any of the details?" Professor Cunningim answered. "And considering what happened, is it likely that someone made them up?

So did the Jesus stories, with their extended metaphors, really occur. As with all histories, that depends on what people remember. And different witnesses remembered the Jesus story differently, as we discover when we compare the various Gospels.

Figuring it out:

After the high drama at the end of Jesus' life, and after the various stories floating around began to be collected, there was still one enormous question, *"What was it all about?"*

Was Jesus the anticipated "Messiah" of the Jews? And if not, who was he? Here were people who claimed to have known him, wandering around the Roman world making preposterous claims about him. Why should anyone take them seriously?

And then, onto the historical scene, came a Jewish pharisee, Saul of Tarsis, a Roman citizen who claimed to have figured out the larger significance of the Jesus story. One day, while traveling on the road to Damascus, "Saul" was overwhelmed by a powerful vision of someone calling himself the Resurrected Jesus, who renamed "Saul" as "Paul," and who told him to get further instructions from a gathering of Jesus' followers in the nearby city.

Out of this experience came Paul's early understanding of what was going on. (The fancy word is "theology.") Based on his experiences with the so-called "Resurrected Jesus," Paul wrote complex explanations of WHAT JESUS WAS ALL ABOUT in the form of letters to the early churches. We call them "St. Paul's Epistles" and parts of them are read every Sunday in most churches. They became the foundation of what we know as "Christianity."

The Metaphorical Church:

Fast forward. Two thousand years later we come to the modern Christian Church, the continuing collection of historical institutions that carry on the Jesus Story. Two thousand years! Doesn't that seem surprising? And the Jesus story that was told in the beginning is essentially the same story we tell today. (Yes, in spite of the Dead Sea Scrolls and the Gnostic Gospels.)

I'm capitalizing the word "Church," because I am referring to all the various churches: Catholic, Protestant, Orthodox, Non-sectarian, Evangelical, Pentecostal, and so forth. It is true, of course, that we have many versions of Christianity. Yes, we have fought wars over the different versions. But every Christian church says the Lords Prayer. Most Christian churches commemorate the Last Supper, the Crucifixion and the Resurrection. Every Christian church uses the same Old and New

Testaments, even though there are slight variations in different versions. Every Christian church honors the Ten Commandments (which, of course, come from the Jewish faith).

And every Christian church is based on the Great Commandment, "You shall love the Lord your God with all your heart and soul and mind, and you shall love your neighbor as yourself." (Also from the Jewish scriptures. But then, Jesus was a faithful Jew. That is something that Christians, to their shame, have often failed to acknowledge.)

The basics of Christianity are still taught and practiced in essentially the same ways that they were in the beginning, principally because of the Church's larger metaphorical teaching, which is a terrific story in itself. *The sublime drama of the Jesus story lives on through the years because of the metaphorical teachings of the Church.*

Why don't I refer to "churches"— plural, with a small "c"? Because we, in our various denominations, are more alike than we are different. And I need to remind our many critics that any fool can call himself or herself a Christian—can, and frequently does. There are no entrance exams.

But it is the beauty and simplicity of our core beliefs as Christians that define us, and to the extent that someone superimposes hateful and violent rhetoric on our lovely metaphors, the rhetoric comes from what a mentor of mine once referred to as "that other place."

Chapter Eight

Beauty, Truth and Goodness

Nothing is good or true unless it is beautiful

How does knowing all this help us to live our lives? Even if we are, as I have suggested, tuned into the Divine, how do we really know what God expects of us? After all, even our church memberships give us different instructions, depending on what church we go to.

So how are we to decide? By reading the Bible?

Well.... yes and no. Here is my personal opinion.

What is the Bible?

The Bible is a collection of writings—of books—about God.

The Bible is not a history book. Or not primarily. Nor is it some sort of divine transcription, dictated by God. None of the scholars whom I respect believe this. Yes, probably the authors of the various books were "inspired" to write as they did. But they wrote about what they knew then, and we now have additional knowledge.

Furthermore the Bible is not a word-for-word behavioral guide. If you read it carefully you will discover that you can "cherry pick" quotations to reinforce what you already believe. Do you believe in beating children? "Spare the rod and spoil the child." Do you own slaves? "Slaves, obey your masters." Pick a behavior you approve of and find a passage that supports it. There are even passages that support mass murder; I'm never quite sure how Bible literalists explain those away.

But if it is not any of those things, what is the Bible is all about?

The Bible is a set of books (a "library") —some historical, some poetical, some fictional, some prophetical, some legal, some mythological— written over a period of many, many centuries as a record of the Hebrew people's evolving understanding of the nature of God, and (in the New Testament) an evolving understanding of the nature and meaning of Jesus of Nazareth.

My favorite seminary teacher, Father Robert Wierenski, once noted that the Bible is a "living document." By that he meant that *each generation has to reinterpret the Bible in light of what humankind has learned since the previous interpretation.*

What's more, we are commanded to worship God. Nowhere do we find a commandment to worship the Bible. We notice this when we observe the way faithful readers take notes in their Bibles. Bibles are not treated the way we treat flags, or sacred objects. Bibles are treated like textbooks, which is what, in fact, they are.

Created in God's Image:

If we are not to cherry pick behaviors from the Bible, how are we to decide what God wants us to do. For many thousands of years our various religions have attempted to answer that question with various rules and examples, and for thousands of years we, in our varieties of humanness, have ignored the various rules and examples.

However, we do know some things about God's nature which can help us to choose our behaviors. A famous theologian once observed that beauty is "primary." That is, nothing is "of God" unless it is beautiful. The poet John Keats observed: "Beauty is Truth, Truth is Beauty. That is all ye know on Earth, and all ye need to know." Mathematicians speak of "beautiful equations." Scientists speak of "beautiful discoveries." The relationship between truth and beauty is understood everywhere.

Early in the last century, C. S. Lewis wrote a science fiction novel called *Out of the Silent Planet* (Scribner reprint edition, 2003). In the first chapter he imagined a space voyage, and he made a startling error. He imagined the Earth, viewed from outer space, as dark and foreboding. But we now know that the Earth is a cosmic jewel, blue and white, shining in the blackness of the airless space-sky. The first astronauts must have been overwhelmed when they first looked backwards at the beautiful planet they had come from.

It turns out that we earthlings are drenched, soaked and immersed in beauty. Only the everyday-ness of experience causes us to take all this beauty for granted. And what's more, the cosmos itself is drenched in beauty. The photographs of distant galaxies are more glorious than we could ever have imagined. When God said "Let there be light," God wasn't just fooling around! Light there was, streaming and exploding and wild with colors. Could all this have happened by chance? The question doesn't deserve an answer. So even if we knew nothing else about our Creator, we can reasonably conclude that God is beautiful.

Beauty and truth:

Too many modern thinkers have tried to turn beauty and truth into relative words. Something is beautiful, they tell us, because our culture says so. The word is meaningless outside of its cultural context. But anyone, anywhere in the world, experiences sunsets as beautiful. We may have individual tastes (God created opinionated individuals) but the beauty of a rose, the beauty of our blue planet, the beauty of a sleeping child, these are universally recognized and loved.

In designing a worthwhile life, I think we could reasonably ask, "Is this beautiful?" Is hatred beautiful? Is warfare beautiful? Is selfishness beautiful? Is reckless sexual behavior beautiful? If not, then perhaps we don't need rules, we need discernment and consciences.

Goodness:

Related to beauty and truth is goodness. I believe that the same things I just said about Beauty and Truth can be said about Goodness. (I am capitalizing here because I believe I am describing God's Nature.) In fact, the famous theologian, Hans Kung, once observed during a lecture that everyone can recognize Goodness. "To say otherwise is sophistry," he said.

Let's think about some famously good people. The Dalai Lama, Eleanor Roosevelt, Desmond Tutu, Mother Teresa, Nelson Mandela. Gentle, kind, funny, loving souls. (I could do a riff on "funny" as a quality of goodness, because I am suspicious of otherwise good people who are grim.)

And how are the rest of us to be good? We are to be "loving." How does that work? We find a description in Chapter Thirteen of St. Paul's First Letter to the Corinthians in the New Testament. Love is patient, modest, kind, selfless, non-vindictive and enduring. Notice that these are not rules. Apparently each of us is supposed to work them out in our own lives.

The Beatitudes:

Jesus uses the word "blessed" to describe goodness. Let me quote a slightly unusual translation (from *The New English Bible, Oxford University Press 1979*) of what we call "The Beatitudes." This contains the most succinct instructions of how we are to try live:

How blest are these who know their need of God; The kingdom of Heaven is theirs.

How blest are the sorrowful; they shall find consolation.

How blest are those of a gentle spirit; they shall have the earth for their possession.

How blest are those who hunger and thirst to see right prevail; they shall be satisfied.

How blest are those who show mercy; mercy will be shown to them.

How blest are those whose hearts are pure; they shall see God.

How blest are the peacemakers; God shall call them his sons.

How blest are those who have suffered persecution for the cause of the right—

the Kingdom of Heaven is theirs.

(Matthew, Ch. 5, v. 3-10)

Growing souls:

As Christians we believe that we are on Earth to grow souls. And the Beatitudes suggest how we are to do this. We notice how totally foreign these "blests" are from the way we normally behave. What wimps we imagine we would be. How scary. How much we would seem to be inviting someone to sock us.

But these are not rules, these are goals. These are ideals towards which humans are to strive. We have examples of sainted souls who seem close to these goals: Mother Teresa comes instantly to mind

It makes a huge (central) difference if you believe you should use the Beatitudes as a yardstick, versus using Donald Trump.

I resist the temptation to editorialize further. We can all look around and observe where pride, self-indulgence, and hardness of heart are taking us. But if we hold Jesus' goals in our hearts and pray for guidance, maybe we can defy the temptations of what St. Paul called "the Principalities and Powers," by which he meant the material world.

The Devil:

Which brings me reluctantly to the subject of evil (again). "Do you have to believe in the Devil," a grandchild once asked me, "if you also believe in God?" My puzzled answer was that I don't know. But if we think of our word "God" as an earthly metaphor, then there would have to be a paradoxical equivalent. (Yes, yes, I know that makes your head hurt. Sorry.)

An evil spiritual entity strikes me as an unnecessary idea. We human creatures have plenty of hateful aggression built into our animal natures without needing a supernatural coach. Still, once we developed complex minds, we got together and combined our individual sinfulness into an actual force that we refer to as "evil." Does that supernatural force then supply energy and ideas? Apparently so.

It does seem true that Evil (capital "E") is more than just the absence of goodness. And Evil is not self-evident in the way that goodness is self-evident; C. S. Lewis taught us that in his book, *The Screwtape Letters* (gift edition: Harper One, March 6, 2001) The Devil often wears attractive clothes, so to speak, and often masquerades as goodness. "But he was such a nice person. Everyone liked him," was said about a pastor who nearly wrecked a church. "Hitler was wonderful with little children," someone later noted about the Nazi leader.

The Devil is seductive. The Devil leads us to death and destruction, but often we don't understand that destruction is where we're headed. the Devil can show up as patriotism. It can show up as obsession with family, as we see with clan warfare in Africa, the Balkans and the Middle East. It can show up as ambition. It can show up as false spirituality. The Devil represents our animal instincts run amok. It shows up as that nasty little voice in our minds telling us to "take care of number one."

Summary:

We experience God's essential nature in the beauty all around us: in the presence of kind, loving people in our lives, and in our instinctive recognition of what is true and good. But in this paradoxical universe we need to be aware of the power of evil as well, particularly when we act out our animal natures in greedy and destructive ways.

Chapter Nine

God In The Details

God is always pursuing us.

I have been talking about ideas that we can consider together. Now I need to get personal. I suppose every person considering himself or herself to be religious has some personal notion about God's reality. And most of us pay lip service to the ideas about God that we learned in church.

But what do we really believe—what do I really believe?

In order to answer that question I need to go back to the idea of "core beliefs." You will recall that I wrote a whole book (*Living As If*, Jossey-Bass 1994) about how our individual ideas influence everything else about us, and how varied these ideas are. As I mentioned earlier, I call these individual ideas our "core beliefs."

Core beliefs may or may not be related to church membership. When you tell me you are an Episcopalian, I don't really know if you believe in

God, miracles, heaven, or even in the Bible. So when a young person expresses confusion about personal faith, as my granddaughter did, I can only say that we each have to find a genuine faith for ourselves. But God will help us if we keep our "radios" turned on.

The idea of God:

Some years ago I spent a night with a favorite cousin in California, whom I almost never have a chance to see. Over a late evening glass of wine, we got to talking about religion. At some point, my cousin's very nice wife said with a smile, "I don't need the idea of God in order to explain things."

I was caught up short by the phrase, "the idea of God."

"I don't think of God as an idea," I said. "I think of God as an experience."

But that explanation, as you can imagine, didn't "compute" with my cousin and his wife. They had, so to speak, no hooks to hang it on. Was I talking about a "born again" experience? No? So what would an "experience" of God be like? It turned out to be impossible to describe.

I recall another friend who once told a newspaper reporter about her sense of God "communicating" with her.

"How do you know it's not just your subconscious talking," the reporter asked.

"I'm very clear about the difference," my friend responded firmly, as though that clarified anything.

Experiencing God:

How does anyone have an experience of God? And why does God bother with us anyway?

We have lots of personal "testimonies" to God's presence in the world. One of my favorites is from Duke University English professor Reynolds Price's little book, *Letters To A Man In the Fire*. (Touchstone 2000). He tells of a vision of encountering Jesus after he (Price) had had terrible cancer surgery. In the vision, they were both standing in the Sea of Galilee, and this "Jesus" person tenderly washed his open wound. Jesus then started to walk away, and Price called after him, "Won't you cure me?" Jesus looked back and said, "That too."

I find testimonies like this, which are a little bit funny, to be more persuasive than impassioned ones. (Price was, much later, cured of cancer, although paralyzed from the waist down.) It seems to me that products of merely wishful thinking would not be funny.

Yes, I too have had encounters that seemed unquestionably to be "of God," and no, I'm not going to tell you about them here. I feel sure that many (maybe most) of you have had similar experiences. I hope you knew or believed enough to recognize whom you were dealing with. (Having been told when we were children that that wasn't really a boogie-man in the nighttime closet, our grownup selves sometimes tend to be skeptical of apparent specters who may be merely imaginary).

The Infinite and Intimate God:

So who is this God whom I and so many others have encountered? For myself, I have two ways of thinking about God. I imagine God the way Huston Smith talks about God in his book, *The Soul Of Christianity* (Harper/SanFrancisco 2005). He refers to God as utterly unimaginable. He uses the word "Infinite." God as Pure, Undivided Love. No parts.

But at the same time, as a Christian, I also think of God as an intimate part of my psyche, influencing my thoughts, answering my questions, consoling me.

How can that be? I am "finite." I am a living animal with physical parts. But in some mysterious way I am also part of the Infinite. My mind seems to be "God imprinted," maybe in the way that geese are "imprinted" by their mothers early in their lives. The Quakers refer to "That of God" in each of us, and to "the Inner Light." Yes. All metaphors for the Great Unknown.

Huston Smith has important things to say on this subject:

> We cannot know the Infinite. Because we are in it, intimations of the Infinite will seep into us occasionally, but more than this we cannot manage on our own. If we are to know it

intimately, the Infinite must take the initiative and show itself to us. If there is to be a love affair between the Infinite and the finite, the Infinite must do the wooing. (p. 12)

God reveals God's self to us, not the other way around. We do not "discover" God through our own limited efforts. This was the problem I was having with my cousin and his wife. If I had said, "God was there for me when I was ready," would that have made sense to them? God chasing after me? But I think my sweet cousin and his sweet wife had better watch out. They are loving people. God may get them yet. Because I believe that God is always pursuing us.

In his poem, "The Hound of Heaven," Francis Thompson puts it this way:

I fled him down the nights and down the days;
I fled him down the arches of the years;
I fled him down the labyrinthine ways
Of my own mind; and in the midst of tears
I hid from him, and under running laughter.
Up vistaed hopes I sped;
And shot, precipitated,
Adown Titanic glooms of chasmed fears,
From those strong feet that followed, followed after.

> But with unhurrying chase,
>
> And unperturbed pace,
>
> Deliberate speed, majestic instancy,
>
> They beat—and a Voice beat
>
> More instant than the Feet—
>
> "All things betray thee, who betrayest Me."

Resistance to God:

Anyone who goes around advocating for God, as I often do, soon discovers that knowledge of God is unlike knowledge of algebra. No matter how logical the argument may seem to me, other people seem to be amazingly stuck in their misguided opinions.

A mentor of mine once used the word "vertigo" to describe how it feels to have your core beliefs challenged. We are all confronted with lives of uncertainty, danger and mystery. So, somewhere in early childhood, most of us unconsciously absorb the beliefs of those around us—parents and teachers in particular. This enables us to feel comfortable in a scary and disorganized personal world. Everything else about us is then based on these unconscious assumptions, which are, as I have described, our Core Beliefs.

Caught by God:

But if God "catches" us, as happened to me, what does that mean?

A number of metaphors have been used. In the Bible, Jesus tells someone that he must be "born again of the Spirit," and that is the phrase used by our fundamentalist brethren. I have heard the word "awakened," and of course, the term "conversion" means "turned around." Saul of Tarsis was knocked down and made blind when the risen Christ appeared to him and turned him into the Apostle Paul. Luckily (or not) most of us will not encounter Jesus in such an unmistakable way.

I think that my own conviction about God's presence resulted from a lowering of my self-important intellect, so that my spiritual radio could take in the messages that had been beamed my way for a long, long time.

So, to return to my two ways of thinking about God, I believe that God is both absolutely "other" and absolutely intimate. When we say that we are "made in the image of God" we are referring, I believe, to the God-in-us, which Carl Jung didn't quite identify with the collective unconscious (not necessarily holy), and which isn't quite the Holy Spirit (not solely part of ourselves), but rather refers to our awed response to the holiness all around us: to every rose petal, every sunset, every thunderstorm. every baby, even every badly performed version of "Messiah" or shaky singing of "Amazing Grace."

Francis Thompson ends his poem like this:

Sarah R. Taggart

Halts by me that footfall :

Is my gloom, after all,

Shade of His hand, outstretched caressingly?

"Ah, fondest, blindest, weakest,

I am He Whom thou seekest !

Thou dravest love from thee, who dravest me."

Epilogue

God at the Fringes of Science

In the previous chapters I have talked about paradigms and about how common sense influences what we are willing to believe. Now I want to talk about some new ideas that flirt with the fringes of what we know scientifically. *Many are just ideas.* That does not mean they are not true, but it does mean they may be hard to understand or to prove. I am putting them here because they are not essential to my basic argument, and I did not want to bog readers down in this complex of speculations.

But for me, they open doors to my belief in God.

No parts:

A friend of mine once observed that we can depend on some facts absolutely. She was talking about mathematics. And it is true that science—genuine science—has depended heavily on mathematics.

But mathematics only applies to realities that have parts—numbers, molecules, activities, etc. Mathematics, after all, is basically the study of relationships. But there are many aspects of reality that seem to have no "parts." Thoughts, for example, or emotions.

Our scientific assumption has always been that before there can be a "happening" there has to be a "thing" to cause it to happen. And "things" have "parts." Things are available to study. For example we had to have brains (a thing) before we could have thoughts. There had to be cosmic dust (things) before there could be primitive life. We have even projected God as a "thing." But if we are not "things," what are we?

Who are we and where did we come from?

Thanks to modern astrophysics (the study of everything in the sky that came after the Big Bang) scientists are no longer so sure they know what kind of Reality is fundamental. Parallel universes, black holes, and invisible matter make many old ideas seem quaint and inadequate. The huge idea about Creation—who we are and where we came from—has changed hugely.

Did life originate on earth? There is now evidence that life came crashing in from outer space—not actual creatures, of course, but the seeds of life, organic matter. Outer space seems to be rich in organic matter, drifting around in cosmic dust and ice. Space, it seems, is not the sterile place we once thought. And for this reason, it seems unlikely that we are alone in the universe.

Nor is space just an empty container for rocky this-and-thats which lumped together seconds after the Big Bang. The more closely scientists are able to examine the universe, the more odd it seems, and the more questions they have. After watching an eye-popping series of gorgeous photographs from outer space, a prominent astrophysicist was asked a whimsical question by a TV interviewer. "If you could ask God one question, what would it be?"

The scientist smiled. "That's easy," he said. "I'd ask, what are we made of? Because, really, we have no idea."

What is matter?

We are taught that we are made of "matter." But how real is matter? Mr. Wise (his actual name), my seventh grade science teacher, once pointed to the table he was standing beside and noted that it looked solid. "Is it really solid?" he asked the class.

We all nodded obediently.

"No," he said, "actually it is mostly empty space. It is loosely filled with thousands of molecules, which are in continuous motion. And inside molecules are atoms, also moving around, and inside atoms are electrons.

What Mr. Wise didn't know then, but we have discovered since, is that inside electrons are quarks, and inside quarks are.what? Primary particles of bizarre kinds? Energy? But what is energy?

We thought we could comprehend what matter was. We could look at it under a microscope, we could take it apart, we could analyze what it was made of, we could tinker with it. We could experiment with the ways in which it changed back and forth, in and out, from energy. Even (look how smart we were) we could release the energy tied up in matter and blow up the world with our atom bombs.

But, in fact, we have no idea about matter itself, that seemingly solid stuff all around us. What actually is matter? There seems to be invisible matter, anti-matter, and who knows what else, in addition to our everyday variety. And when matter is taken apart, down to the tiniest particles, suddenly these tiny particles behave in extremely unpredictable and unlikely ways, seemingly influenced by whatever questions the researcher is posing at that moment. Solid matter seems to dissolve into what is called "uncertainty".

TEMS:

Maybe it isn't true that matter is fundamental. Maybe matter is merely is one function of a larger reality. Energy is another function. Time is a third function. Space is a fourth function. These four, together, are referred to by some New Age thinkers as TEMS. A physicist friend objects that this is not a scientific term, but whether or not it is accepted science, it is an idea that challenges old fashioned thinking.

TEMS refers to Time-Energy-Matter-Space as a single, interactive phenomenon. Let's give other names to these familiar ideas. Matter can refer to "pattern." Energy can refer to "motion." Time can refer to "velocity." Space can refer to "volume." So perhaps it was TEMS that was created by the Big Bang—the whole package, not just matter and energy.

Think about it. Any aspect of TEMS will be changed by change in any other aspect, and you can't have any one without the other three. It is a classic "system." When Einstein first pointed this out, everyone thought he was crazy. But we know now that the interrelationship between time, energy, matter and space is fundamental to everything about reality.

But is this all? Where, then, is Life? And where is "consciousness"? Does any aspect of TEMS do any "thinking"? Not as far as we know. So where did thinking come from?

"From chemistry," the scientists tell us, "along with the rest of the above."

As if that explains anything.

Non-locality:

Here is a basic idea that connects science and religion. As we discussed earlier, apparently everything in Creation is connected. It begins to look like there are no "separate parts." Everything influences everything. So when you ask, "How can God be everywhere at once?" we now have a scientific answer.

Particle physicists recently made a discovery called the Einstein-Podosky-Rosen theory. It seems that once a pair of primary particles are spinning in opposite directions from each other, each will change direction when the other one does, *even when they are far apart in space*. The word that scientists use is "non-local." Apparently we live in a "non-local" universe. Everything is connected to everything, not in the way that wheels are connected to cars, nor radio waves are connected to broadcast towers, but in the way that light goes everywhere.

It seems that we live in an enormous interactive, interconnected "field." This, of course, is what our religious faith teaches us. We are all connected to each other and to God. When we pray for someone's health, sometimes they get better. How does this work? Maybe this is how.

Process before product:

We have already observed that we are not "things." but rather are living creatures with souls. But what on earth does that mean? Now don't be bowled over by this explanation. It really is quite simple. And crucially important if we are to believe in souls.

It is an old theory, coming to us from the ancient Eastern religions. The idea is that "process" (the idea) precedes "product" (the result). Always. Before there were computers (products), Bill Gates and Steve Jobs were thinking and creating (process). Which leads to the gigantic, all-encompassing idea that before there was the Big Bang (product),

God's Conscious Will existed (process). Some Asian religions refer to "Ultimate Mind." That is not what we mean by our word "God" (we experience a God who is in relationship with us) but it is certainly one way to think about the "otherness" of God.

Perhaps the ultimate Creator thought about us before creating us and becoming one of us. Wonderful. And what did "Creation" consist of? The creation of "parts." The "Great Unity" (God) exploded into millions and billions and gazillions of parts. In other words, God created TEMS, the building blocks of the Universe.

Or at least, that's one way of thinking about it.

LaVergne, TN USA
15 February 2010
173133LV00008B/13/P